HEALING AND OTHER FUTILE ENDEAVOURS

POEMS

By Cliff Turner

Once, as a child,
I spent several minutes
trying to lift a board
that I was standing on
thinking I could fly.

Contents

Descend

It never leaves, you know. That dull ache in the pit of your stomach, that gnawing, that haunting itch of something dying. It will always be there. If you've tasted the bitterness on the floor of your soul, you will never be rid of it. If you don't know what I speak of, then you've not yet been there. If you do, then welcome. My words will not be able to help you. But in that is the hidden beauty. Once a spirit is torn it creates a new, terrifyingly beautiful creature. The best and worst of its host writhing together in a grotesque, sensual mass of potential. Nothing from without can affect its course at that point. No wise words, no platitudes, no song or food or action can reach in and destroy or change it. No, it will dwell in you, as much a part of you as any necessary organ. Draw from it fear or power, that is your choice. The choice of the host. Wear it as an albatross or a crown. Feed it to your days as a poisonous toxin or a miracle tonic. But know that its essence will not be altered. Your only hope, if you have been to the birthplace of this blasphemous creature, is to embrace its power. Allow it to eat your fear, for it certainly can. Live through the courageousness it possesses. For it will not be denied, and nor shall you.

Oblivion

It's dark.
It's quiet.
I remember jumping.
I remember falling.
Beyond that,
I remember nothing.
Only some remnant of guilt.
I should be confused,
But I'm not.
Just oddly construed.

So what happens now?
I half expect Persephone,
Or the River Styx.
But I wholly know,
This dark is all there is.

3 AM

3 AM
12 years old
Mom pulled us,
my sister and I,
from our beds.
Now safe in the car.
Away from the jackals.
A man we trusted,
and his friends.
Drunken terrors.
Unspeakable demands.
But …
She'd forgotten her purse.
"Don't come in"
"No matter what"
She stormed back inside.
And we cried.

Please, Daddy

Daddy burned the house down
I was in bed when his match was lit
After a night of yelling about it
Frantically pacing
His footsteps booming below my bedroom
His barking shouts
His audible, desperate grin
Making me flinch again and again
Uncontrollable tears
He said he can't handle it anymore
Her memory
Her ghost
It was either him or the house
He came and got me at least
The orange glow is behind us now
I can see it in the side mirror
I cough and cry
I choke
My throat raw with smoke
His eyes raw with emptiness
Please, Daddy, please
Keep this car on the road

Snake Oil from the Worms

Come on, step beyond
It's better here than there
Or practically anywhere
It's soothing, it's calm
There is no one to miss you
When you are gone
An oak and satin home
Granted, a bit earthy
Your spot marked with stone
We won't leave you all alone
Come on, step beyond

A Regression of Questions

It wasn't so much about "Why"
Not anymore. "Purpose" had lost its import
Though, she did ask on odd occasion
Out of curiosity or remorse

Neither was it about "How"
Her plans had a habit of abandonment
So, reluctantly releasing the reins
She escaped their testament

Now, it's more about "What" and "When"
Allowing the traffic lights of life to rule
Time dictating her momentum
Reacting only to what intrudes

Broken Glass

The taste of broken glass was in my mouth
        before I walked in the room.

Her soul was about to leave, to abandon her body
        on that clinical slab of a bed.

Her three stood by her side but their souls felt
        more dead than she.

Her husband stood empty, his spirit collapsed in a heap,
        muttering in confusion, lost.

Her boy quivered with fear. His world about to change.
A void to appear
        that he dreaded to face.

But her girl!
Oh her girl!
Her girl destroyed me.

They expected eloquent words and powerful prayers.
"Help us preacher-man!"
        their souls screamed at me, echoing in my
emptiness.

I'd faced demons and pain and death and came through.
But nothing prepared me for her girl.

I'd been in the presence of pure evil, had it seep through
my bones.
But nothing prepared me for her girl.

The broken glass hit a crescendo as she did it. Her soul
shredded and cried
a cry of pain far worse than anything I had ever
felt.

A billion sorrows gushed from her spirit which lay
writhing
on the floor in it's deepest despair.

Then,
she smiled.

She looked into her mother's eyes and smiled. She gave
her mother permission
to go with that smile.

The girl's soul found no comfort in it. Her spirit cried it's
loudest
as her mother left.

Yet,
           she smiled.

I've felt horror and pain in others that shook my
existence. This preacher-man thought
           he could handle anything.

But nothing prepared me
           for her girl.

If The Darkness Had Teeth

If the darkness had teeth
I would welcome it with ease
For then there would be scars
Scabs to pick at and bleed

But instead it is dull
Bringing only what is numb
It's passiveness frustrating
A drumming hum in my skull

Bite! Lash out!
Flood the emotional drought
Just make me feel something
Or what is life about?

The Chain

Every day he would pull at the chain
Every day strength built in his four legs
Every day he would exhaust himself again

Pulling!
      Snapping!
           Running!
               Panting!
                    Straining!
                        Raging!

It was an ordinary day when the chain broke
When he looked around and then lay down
Because he didn't know where to go

Trauma

    She wore it
Like a comfortable old sweater
A shield from damp responsibility
Insulation from cold fault and onus
The warm sweet hug of martyrdom

    As any favourite sweater
Comfortable and familiar within
Its intimacy blinding to the truth
Threadbare, frayed and pilled
For those who would carefully look

    Yet she wore it
Woven ever-ready excuses
Buttons tight to reality's breeze
No one pulled the first thread, so
She blended seamlessly with the wool

You Can Always Check Out

It's been a lot of nights
This hotel is not so bad I guess
The breakfast is always warm
The sheets get changed
There's clean water in the pool
What more can you ask for really?

It gets a bit old though
The same room, the same halls
Kind of forgotten why I'm here
I could go but I don't know where
Besides, there are two people in the next room
They're used to me being around

Guess I'll see how it goes
Maybe something will change
New candies in the vending machine?
A friendly new server in the lounge?
It can't just stay the same forever, can it?
Can it?

The clerk tells me I can check out
But I can't check back in.
Guess it's a once in a lifetime kind of thing.
Suppose I'll give it another day
There are new towels in the shower
So there's that

Leaving Life

Thick mist —- Silhouette
You wave —- Nothing yet

"Who's there?" —- Motionless
Cold air —- "What is this?"

Slight turn —- Slow steps back
"Follow?" —- "Is it that?"

They wave —- Finally
Point north —- Right this way

"Where to?" —- Just silence
"Alright." —- Compliance

They walk —- You behind
No words —- Faceless, blind

Engulfed —- In that fog
Wordless —- Epilogue

You turn —- Others there
In place —- Where you were

Thick mist —- Silhouette
They wave —- Nothing yet

This Idea

This idea
This philosophy
This temptation of uncharted action
Dances seductively before me
Her hips revolve and sway
Hypnotic, tantalizing movements
Glass promises of a flawless outcome

If only
She was a woman
Resisting her lustiness would be simple
But this idea
This philosophy
This temptation of uncharted action
Has established an amorous grip

And now
The brink of endeavour
Is she an angel, siren or aphrodisiac?
Shall I most fear change or stagnation?
This idea
This philosophy
This temptation of uncharted action

No matter … I am seduced

Evolve

Grappling with the creature born at the death of your own innocence is a hideous experience overflowing with potential. Thoughts repressed or embryonic rise to their newfound freedom and alight the electric pathways of your conscious mind. Possibility presents itself from every angle and each direction adjacent to them yet again. Infinitely constellating alternatives. Overwhelming, yes, for each possibility consists of light and dark, "good" and "evil", productivity and disaster. At this point, you are omniscient for a moment barely long enough to sense. The questions you ask in this moment, as your scorched soul squirms screaming on the floor, will define your eternal record. Time moves only forward, and each action and thought will be as they were for eternity. So it is of the greatest import that your ragged soul, tortured by happenstance and disturbed decisions of others, fight mightily against that grotesque beast born in trauma. You, in your depths, have the power and undeniable right to become what is needed. To become a creature more terrifying than that beast. To consume and assimilate it. Then rise anew in the glory of what you have become in the wake of your shattered soul. Be it dark. Be it light. This matters not. It simply must be.

Coffee with God

God sits across from me
Sipping coffee
Eyes slipping blankly
To the napkin between her fingers
Stroking, folding, fidgeting

She's been silent
Since the coffee was hot
Adrift in her thoughts
Unnoticed, unrecognized, almost lost
Where goes the mind of a god?

Suddenly a spark
Her eyes rise to meet mine
Her lips begin to part
But settle back to silence
Leaving me still in the dark

Standing she buttons her coat
Walks to the door
Leaving me exposed, alone
She vaguely says to no one
"I forget what I built this for"

My Father Lives in the Attic

My father lives in the attic
At least, that's what I've been told
They left me a note that explains it all
To some degree I suppose

The note says I'll be safe
As long as I believe he's there
It says he's watching out for me
But he's never come downstairs
I can't find a way up
But they say he's waiting for me there

No one ever brings him food
I hear no footsteps or signs of life
They say I can speak to him through the vents
But I've never heard his voice
"Believe he is there and you'll be safe" says the note
"Stop believing? He'll burn the house and end your life"

My father lives in the attic
At least, that's what I've been told

Awaken!

From what?

Awaken from the numb
Awaken to what you seek
Awaken to what you run from
Feel your tightly wound sheets

I didn't know I was asleep

Awaken to simplicity
Awaken to chaos
Awaken to your eccentricity
Free your neck of its albatross

I prefer slumber in my darkened box
Here I am warm
Here I am safe
Here I don't need to take any form

Awaken, take shape
Awaken to love
Awaken to the fact that you hate
Transform into what you've become

But I am afraid

Awaken

Fitted Sheet

It's always the damned fitted sheet,
Causing an existential crisis.
Oh sure, it fits delightfully tight on my bed,
But it's disgustingly difficult to fold.
I simply want to store it away for another day.
Why does it insist on causing such chaos?
Why did I consent to own such a catastrophe?
Do I depend upon such complicated possessions?
Is comfort this crucial?
Do I belong to that weak of a species?
Creating objects of comfort and convenience.
Typically complicating and convoluting life all the more.
Like this frustrating fitted sheet!
So we work, we earn (as our years quickly burn)
To purchase objects that preoccupy our time.
Attain them to maintain them and later complain of them.
Is this what we are here for?
Is this the point of it all?
To create complexity in search of ease and comfort?
Can our consciousness not transcend this?
It's always the damned fitted sheet.

That Void

"Fill it with liquor" say the barkeeps
"Fill it with sex" say the lonely

That void
Jumping between soul and stomach
Seeking, yearning, longing
For something bigger, deeper, warmer

"Fill it with wealth" say the capitalists
"Fill it with duty" say the socialists

But contentment is the realm
Of beasts and gods
To be human is to ache
To forever fail to appease
That void

"Fill it with goods" say the merchants
"Fill it with faith" say the preachers

That void
So much advice
Like fingers in a dam
But whose voids do these fill?

Inner Voice

My body is mine but not me.
Simply a conveyance for consciousness.
That, I understand.
My dilemma is the voice within.
Talking incessantly.
An unceasing dialogue in my head.
As I am awake,
Calculating, justifying, scheming.
Dreaming while asleep.
My conundrum with this constant conversation is:
Am I the speaker,
Or is it speaking to me?

Vortex

His tail, is it always fluffy like that?
I've never seen a squirrel when I wasn't there.

The words you speak.
Are they the same when I'm not aware?

Do smiles persist
After I've walked away?

Does the world appear on my approach
And collapse in my wake?

Is it an abyss?
And my consciousness is the existence snare?

His tail, is it always fluffy like that?
I've never seen a squirrel when I wasn't there.

Argument in Delusion

"She's not here!" His own neurons fired at He.

"Why can't She be?" He said to He, "That's She! Can't You see? Just let Me be so We can flee. Real or mystery, this is key to Me; to be with She!"

"But Me," He said to He,
"I am only thinking of Her eyes and thighs, all the while I die inside. Time flies by with no respite and no sign of Her shine in my life."

"No!" He roared from and at His own soul,
"How abhorrent You are to implore Me to destroy what makes Me whole! Go now! Cajole Me no more. Allow My slow revolt and Her cosmic glow to grow!"

Either defeated or conceded, His neurons retreated. And She was with He finally.

Spider Thought

The thought flitted then lit upon me
Not quick like a hypnagogic kick
But slick like the tickle of a spider
Clicking slowly, each step flicking into view
A bit of knowledge dripping a trail of shame
Now it sits in plain sight, lit by my wick
Cynically grinning at me it spits,

"Knowledge is a sword, the unknown hydra.
One learned swipe births several more unknowns.
Silence is the realm of the wise."

Sheep's Teeth

Sheep's teeth,
the facade with which I eat my meals.
    A diet of meat
        and frustration.
Mastication is a gnawing,
        a grinding.
The cuts set before me are not intended for these ...
        these dull hammers of teeth.

Others at the table, they dine sharp.
    With incisors of cats, dogs,
        lions.
Rending, tearing.
Meat opening before them,
    easily shredded,
        gulped.

My sheep's wool entangles me,
    my opportunity.
Bleating I fear my sharp toothed duality.
    Though my Cerberus longs
        to be unleashed,
            to destroy the dining room
            and all within.

There is no middle for me
        you see.

                It's sheep or unholy monster.

And so,
        the wool defies the teeth.

                Perhaps it's time …
                        time for a shearing.

Cry?

A girl who couldn't hold her tears inside.
She cried, she cried, kind of tried but still cried.

With one shift she found an uneasy peace.
Her mind cleared, her tears ceased.

Now her presence has evaporated.
She's unseen, she's unheard, unbelieved, undetected.

A new pain, no better or worse, but dry.
To exist and subsist as a mist? Or to cease to resist
and just … cry?

Arise

So now what have you become? A creature born out of the depths of despair? A monstrosity of power developed through torturous experience? An angelic beast of fury and love? No matter, here you are. Standing at the gates of a world that will refuse to accept you in any form. Only to find that in the pockets of life in which answers are expected, more questions will be found. The certainty of uncertainty is the only conduit for your power now. To bathe gleefully in the unpredictability and chaotic beauty of our tumultuous society. Pour your essence into the churning mix of uncountable perfumes and revel in the difference it makes. For, the second you attempt to solidify any conclusion or idea, it will rebel and slip further into a gaseous state, taunting you all the while. Your power, found in the darkest place, as robust and strong as it is, will never be enough to harness meaning. But it is more than powerful enough to sustain you as you explore meaninglessness and all the possibilities therein.

Etcetera

Where now? Her purpose …
Fulfilled. Her goals …
Met or abandoned. Her life …
Far from over. Her path …
Freedom. To walk …
Into the etcetera …

etc …

etc …

etc …

Conjecture

Conjecture, my friend.
It's just what it is. Isn't it?

In our ever growing accession to information
facts have been mired in myth.
Possession of truth is a colluded delusion
and factuality lost to an abyss.

A chaotic churning of mismatched learning
stirred by those who imply denial.
Each knowing infinitely less than the next
fearing the truth's rumoured arrival.

It's on quicksand we stand, havoc in hand.
with no firmament to cement our ascent.
So then how do we assess and define progress
when truth eludes the best of intent?

Conjecture, my friend.
It's just what it is. Isn't it?

In The Grey

Waves rush forcefully from shore
Crashing away from certainty in the partially known
Charcoal from one coast
Snow from the other
They journey toward centre
And calm to a slow roll
Meeting, swirling, blending
Creating a multitude of shades
In the grey

Some are afraid to swim here
In the grey
Afraid to flee the safety of their noisy clans on shore
But strong swimmers move freely
In the grey
Knowing nothing is fully known
And little completely unknown
Swimming in confident possibility
In the grey

Focus

It's hard to see
That middle part

Sure…

The microscopic is easy
Zoom in on the minute
Ruminate there
Burden it with worries
"That phase from yesterday
Spoken all wrong"

The same for the macro
Stand back to observe
The overarching scheme
To judge without meaning
"Oh silly humanity
When will we learn?"

But …

In that middle part lay
Consequence and responsibility
Foggy and grey
And damn,
It's hard to see

Two Angels and A Witch

I sat with the witch for coffee
as we had done many times before
Our conversation was as it was
We touched on nothing and everything
The usual chat of two people
With worlds we hide just because

But the thoughts grew rabid
They gnawed out of their cages
The witch and I were powerless
to the force that was so long at bay
the sensing of life and death
the ending of existence blessed

With gentleness we scarred our minds
The witch lamented her vision
While I yearned to know what she saw
We spoke of another universe
The true power of love purely made
But conclusions weren't ours to draw

In the presence of the witch I met two angels
Their embrace destroyed us both
Light broke through the ground
And within us hope awoke

Just a Shift

I hate doing the dishes
           I had food to dirty them

I have to make my bed
           I have a bed to sleep in

My friends are annoying me again
           I have friends who care

It is such a long way to walk
           I am able to walk there

Spaghetti

It's not a matter of "How" … No
   It's about spaghetti
It's about clock hands waving angrily
   and batteries drowning
      in their own sullen thoughts
It's about a jam you can never have
   because
      tomorrow always becomes today
It's about a distant piano
   and the wrong boots on a muddy path;
      forever haunting
   It's about rain and pudding
It's about the cyclops camera
   winking frantically in stop motion
      with its irrelevant judgements
It's about "what a loser," and "get a grip"
   and "get it right, you stupid kid"
It's about paper ships
   singing their way into a whirlpool
      praying for oblivion
   It's about a low E string
It's about an omnipresent chickadee
   and the smell of fish;
      surprising on a summer afternoon
      … No
It's definitely not a matter of "How"

Wise Sky

The child asked the sky,
"Why are we born to die?
Why try?
Why strive through a lifetime
only to face demise?
Does life's prize evade my mind?
Can you, oh kind sky,
guide me to not simply survive,
but to thrive?
Do you surmise with your wise eye
that life is mine to opine and design?
Might I climb and fly,
and be entertained by
the delights that life provides
before the required goodbye?"

"I do not know,"
the sky replied.
"For you are human and I am sky.
Unlike you, I do not die."

Dubious Conclusion of a Former Preacher

You were born from mystery
You will die to the same
Between you will accumulate
   and speculate
        regurgitate
     what you postulate
Religions and beliefs
they too are born and die
All that remains is
   to accept the uncertain
     enjoy what is before you
       give love to those you love
         show kindness to all
           and
know that there is no control
of the ultimate transition.
   As with us all ...
You were born from mystery.
You will die to the same.

Final Note

In the end, at the wasteland's border where life attempts to find meaning, there is but a vague palette of grey. And in that, is beauty.

The End

Healing and Other Futile Endeavours